RAILWAY HISTORY IN PICTURES: NORTH-WEST ENGLAND

A Lancashire & Yorkshire Railway Manchester-Blackpool express on Walkden troughs hauled by one of Aspinall's 'Atlantics'. The 'Highfliers', as they were dubbed, were the largest inside cylinder engines in the country at the time of their introduction: forty were built at Horwich between 1899 and 1902. Note the unusual headcode provision for two lamps side by side on top of the smokebox

RAILWAY HISTORY IN PICTURES

North-West England

J. ALLAN PATMORE

JOHN CLARKE

DAVID & CHARLES : NEWTON ABBOT

7153 4274 6

Printed in Great Britain by
Bendles (Torquay) Limited
for David & Charles (Holdings) Limited
South Devon House Newton Abbot Devon

CONTENTS

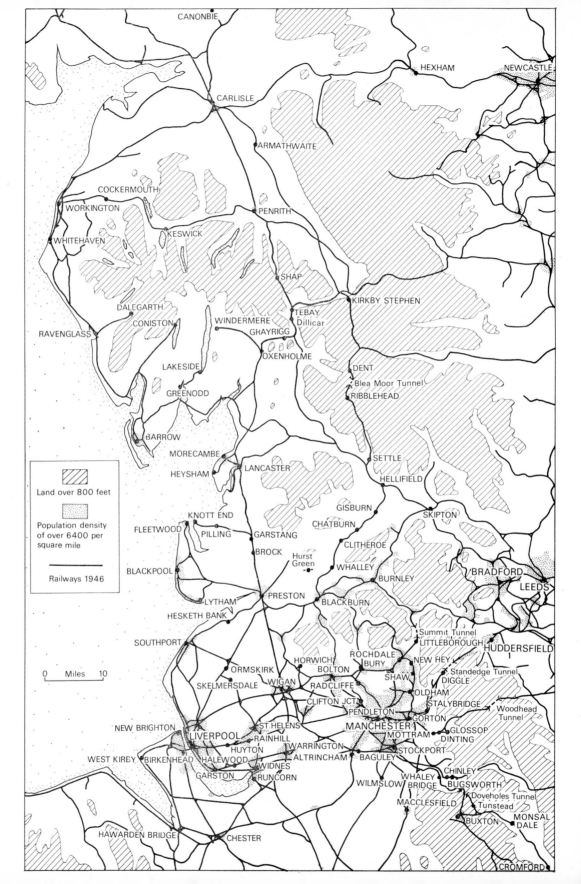

INTRODUCTION

Railways have many fascinations. The fast-dying pulse of steam, the sleek, swift trains of modern-isation, the intricacies of control, the architectural and engineering legacies of a Victorian past, all these and more claim their devotees. The theme of this collection is the railway in its setting, its aim to capture something of the distinctive character of the railway in the North West and of the landscapes to which in turn it gave rise. The emphasis is not so much on the motive power and equipment of the companies which built the routes, for few of them were confined to the North West alone: a Midland express at the approaches to Manchester or Carlisle is no different, save in the details of its background, from a similar train at the approaches to Bristol, Leeds or St Pancras. Rather it is the routes themselves which are distinctive; Peak Forest and Blea Moor belong indubitably to the North West in a way which Mangotsfield, Holbeck or Trent Junction never can.

The boundaries of the area owe more perhaps to publisher's convenience than geographical con-viction, but there is a unity if not a uniformity in that area of England north of Crewe and west of the Pennine watershed. Both authors have lived and worked within its bounds and come to love its railways and their diverse heritage. The selection of views is inevitably personal. In a region so rich in railway history, choice of both theme and illustration is intensely difficult and a reasonable balance hard to achieve. Locomotive engineering or railway architecture, commercial development or social interest, countryside or conurbation, Liverpool or Manchester, Midland or North-Western—the list is endless, but the ultimate selection tries to tell a consistent story within the limits of the allotted space.

My initial ideas for this book came to fulfilment only when happy chance brought me into contact with John Clarke. His technically superb and amazingly numerous and varied photographs of the railway scene in the North West were the foundation on which the present collection is based. His enthusiastic co-operation spurred the work through to completion, and to him I owe a special debt of gratitude. If mine are the words, the melody belongs to him alone. It is sad indeed that his tragic and untimely death on 28 March 1968 robbed him of the opportunity of enjoying these pages in print and took from his many friends a gifted and lively companion.

Oxton
Birkenhead

J. ALLAN PATMORE
Easter 1968

(*Left*) The railway network of the North West at the end of the second world war. The names are an index to places shown in the illustrations. (Railways based, with permission, on the Ordnance Survey. Crown copyright reserved.)

THE RAILWAY AND THE NORTH-WEST SCENE

Railways really began in the North West. With a fitting sense of occasion, the opening of the Liverpool & Manchester Railway on 15 September 1830 was graced by the Duke of Wellington, as Prime Minister, travelling in a special eight-wheeled coach which 'rather resembled an Eastern pavilion than anything our northern ideas considered a carriage . . . and might for magnitude be likened to the car of Juggernaut'. Before and behind were 'two others on a smaller scale, of similar form and workmanship . . . the whole being led by a neat open box, containing a band of music'. The **Northumbrian**, with George Stephenson in charge, headed the train: at 10.40 am, a gun signalled the start of the proud and colourful procession. The events of the opening day need no retelling, but the significance of this line's success, marrying for the first time all the basic elements of the modern railway, can scarcely be over-emphasised. 'Speed - despatch - distance - are still relative terms, but their meaning has totally changed within a few months' wrote Henry Booth, a vigorous promoter of the line and its first historian. 'What was distant is now near. . . Our notions of expedition, though at first having reference to locomotion, will influence . . . the whole tenor and business of life. . . . The traveller will live double times.'

But the influence of the railway was not confined to the traveller alone. As Arthur Bryant wrote, 'the iron horse, with its towering, belching funnel and its long load of roaring coaches plunging through culvert and riding viaduct . . . did not go from village to village: it went from industrial town to town'. The arteries of an urban, industrial revolution, it dominated the urban landscape as it made possible the prosperity of its teeming mills. Nowhere was this more true than in Lancashire. King Cotton was the chief avenue to individual wealth: by the middle of the nineteenth century, it represented nearly a third of the nation's trade and Manchester bid fair to become its commercial hub. From that hub, the railways radiated out, the scale of their works matching the scale of their importance, for the industrial North West was both a product of the railway and a stimulus to its growth. At Stockport in 1842, the Manchester & Birmingham Railway viaduct strides majestically over the infant Mersey as vestiges of an older, rural England are submerged before the engulfing tide of chimneyed mill and terraced house.

Today, much of the landscape of the old industrial North West still remains, despite an ever-accelerating rate of economic and technological change. The scene at Stalybridge in 1967 (left) is rooted in another age. Yet 'dark Satanic mills' give way to the new industry of trading estate and refinery, steam to the electric motor and diesel engine.

Industry alone is far from the sum of the North West. The area has its rich acres of pasture and of ploughland, while to the north and east it is encompassed by striding fell and moorland stream. To the railway builder, dour uplands were an obstacle to his progress, exacting penalties of cost and time. The first Woodhead tunnel cost £200,000 and the lives of twenty-five men and was seven years in the building. Its ultimate successor, seen above in the final phases of construction, cost £4,250,000 and took four years to its completion in 1953. The railways of the North West fascinate in the variety of their setting as in the intricacies of their story.

CANALS & TRAMWAYS

As in many other parts of the country, the earliest railways in the North West were simple tramways employing horse- and cable-haulage, and built as adjuncts to the existing canal network. In Thomas Telford's words of 1800, such 'iron railways' were preferable to a canal navigation 'in countries whose surfaces are rugged, or where it is difficult to obtain water for lockage, where the weight of the articles of produce is great in comparison with their bulk, and where they are mostly to be conveyed from a higher to a lower level'.

The Preston & Walton Summit Plateway was built to link the northern and southern sections of the Lancaster Canal across the deeply incised valley of the Ribble, thus saving the expense and difficulties of a major aqueduct or heavy lockage. Opened in 1803, it was four and a half miles long, but the double transhipment of goods it made necessary was an obvious hindrance in operating the canal. The flood-plain of the Ribble was reached by inclined planes at each end, and was crossed to the south of the river by an embankment which still remains (left). The river was crossed by a timber trestle bridge: the date of the photograph (below) is uncertain, but was probably taken not long after the closure of the line in 1864, and shows a wooden structure on the bridge apparently connected with cable haulage.

The Peak Forest Tramway was an excellent example of a feeder carrying mineral traffic through country too difficult for canal construction. It ran from the Peak Forest Canal at Bugsworth for about seven miles by way of Chapel-en-le-Frith to limestone quarries at Doveholes, with branches to other quarries, reaching a height of 1,139 ft at Loads Knowle. Opened in 1796, it was not finally abandoned until 1921. Loaded wagons were worked down to Bugsworth by gravity, with a brakesman riding on the axle pin of one of the leading wagons (above). The wagons, with flangeless wheels running on flanged rails, had a capacity of two to three tons. One is preserved in York Railway Museum. The abandoned line of the tramway is seen (below) where it runs alongside the former LNWR Buxton line at Barmoor Clough; the stone blocks which supported the rails are still in place along this section.

The bleak uplands of the High Peak are obviously unsuitable country for canal building, but in 1825 the Cromford & High Peak Railway was authorised to link the Cromford and Peak Forest Canals, its chief object in Joseph Priestley's words of 1831 being 'to open a nearer and more convenient communication between the counties of Derby, Nottingham and Leicester, with the port of Liverpool, and the towns of Manchester and Stockport'. It was laid out like a canal, near-level stretches, often sharply curved, being separated by inclined planes instead of flights of locks. From the Cromford Canal, six inclined planes lifted it a total of 990 ft to a summit level of 1,271 ft above sealevel: it then dropped 740 ft by a further three planes to the Peak Forest Canal at Whaley Bridge.

The canal basin at Whaley Bridge is now filled with pleasure craft (above) but the transit shed remains, though its present use (left) is in stark contrast to its initial purpose!

Unlike other tramroads, much of the Cromford & High Peak was subsequently incorporated into a full-scale railway. Steam working began in 1833, though horse-haulage persisted on the stretches between the inclines until 1841. The line was leased by the LNWR in 1861, and formally amalgamated with that company in 1887. In the early 1890s, fundamental changes were made. The section between Hindlow and Parsley Hay was re-aligned, and incorporated into a new line from Buxton to Ashbourne. The section from Parsley Hay to Cromford (High Peak Junction) remained as a steam-hauled line with intervening cable-worked inclines. The short section from Hindlow to Ladmanlow was realigned as a spur to serve quarries and other sidings, but the section from Ladmanlow to Whaley Bridge was abandoned completely except for a short stretch at the Whaley Bridge end.

The photograph shows the abandoned section at the north end of Burbage tunnel, which was closed on 25 June 1892. The tunnel, some 580 yd long, was situated on the summit section of the line, and this view gives some indication of the wild moorland it traversed.

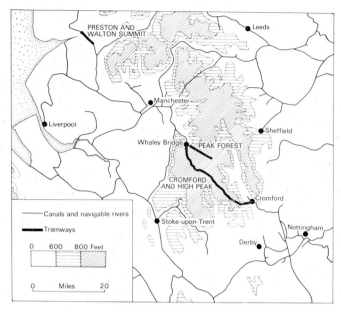

Some of the inclines of the initial alignment were subsequently eased to make continuous locomotive working possible over longer stretches. The most noted in this respect was Hopton incline (right) where locomotives began handling traffic in 1877. When operated by a stationary engine and cable, the whole of the 457 yd incline was graded at 1 in 14, but for locomotive working the lower portions were eased somewhat, only the final 200 yd remaining at this pitch. It was nevertheless the steepest gradient worked by adhesion in Britain. This section of the C & HP saw its final trains on 30 April 1967.

Middleton incline remained cable-worked until its closure on 31 May 1963. It was 708 yd in length, with a gradient of 1 in 8¼, and for all its life, the winding engine was a low-pressure condensing beam type built in 1825. The photograph looking down the incline in December 1937, shows two of the water tanks used on the C & HP to convey water from Cromford for both locomotive and domestic purposes on the dry limestone uplands. The nearest one is built on the frame of a four-wheeled McConnell tender.

The motive-power of the C & HP has been almost as distinctive as its route. The Webb-designed 2—4—0 'Chopper' tanks came on the scene in the 1890s, and one of the class, LNWR 2278, had a particularly long association with the line. It was finally withdrawn in March 1952 as BR 58092 and the last of its class: it spent its final years working between Sheep Pasture Top and Middleton Bottom, where it is seen on 5 June 1950 (top).

North London 0—6—0 tanks came to the line in 1931, and with their high power output and short wheelbase were particularly suited to conditions on the C & HP. 58860, with BR number but still lettered LMS, climbs Hopton incline with water tanks for Hopton on 5 June 1950 (centre). The gradient post on the left marks the transition from 1 in 20 to 1 in 14.

The final workings were in the hands of ex-WD J 94 0—6—0 saddle tanks. 68012 shunts water tanks at Middleton Top on a wintry day in March, 1965 (bottom).

LIVERPOOL & MANCHESTER

The close trading links between the Port of Liverpool and Manchester, the commercial centre of industrial Lancashire, have inspired important innovations in the search for more efficient means of transport between them. The Mersey & Irwell Navigation, an early example of its kind; the Bridgewater Canal, the first major component of the canal network which served the transport needs of the early phases of the Industrial Revolution; the Manchester Ship Canal, the only British ship canal of any size; the East Lancs Road, one of the few completely new motor roads built before 1939—all these were memorable works of their period. But pride of place between the Mersey and Manchester must go to the Liverpool & Manchester Railway, whose thirty miles of route, opened with due pomp on 15 September 1830, were the world's first railway in the full sense of the term. Indeed, it is scarcely too much to claim, with the line's centenary historian, that 'the Liverpool & Manchester Railway showed the world what could be done, and led to the greatest change in the habits of mankind that has ever come about otherwise than by a process of slow and gradual evolution'.

At Liverpool, the relatively high-level direct approach from the east, which the company adopted to overcome Parliamentary opposition to George Stephenson's earlier more northerly route, made the initial passenger terminus at Crown Street more than a mile from the centre of the town and over 150 ft above it. First class passengers were conveyed by omnibus to Dale Street in the city centre; the vehicles can be seen on the left in this Ackermann print of 1831. All trains were cable-hauled over the short distance through the tunnel from Edge Hill.

The railway was carried into Manchester on a masonry viaduct across the Irwell (on the left in this Ackermann print): this led to the curious layout at the Liverpool Road terminus, where the platform level was at the upper floor of the terminal building. Unlike those at Crown Street, these buildings still survive (see page 70) though the bridge at the right over Water Street was replaced about 1910.

A centenary recollection of the Rainhill trials of 1829, when the effectiveness of steam traction was convincingly demonstrated. The Henry Ford replica of Stephenson's **Rocket** in its original condition is seen displayed on St George's Plateau, Liverpool, in September 1929 before being shipped to the USA. In the background is part of the facade of Alfred Waterhouse's North Western Hotel, completed in 1870.

19

The country between Liverpool and Manchester offers few major obstacles to railway construction, but the route ultimately chosen meant crossing sandstone ridges at Rainhill and Olive Mount. The former was surmounted by 'inclined planes' with gradients of 1 in 96, but at Olive Mount Stephenson chose to maintain a virtually level route, involving the excavation of almost half a million cubic yards of rock in creating a sheer-sided cutting over eighty feet in depth and almost two miles in length. Alfred Clayton's lithograph shows the cutting shortly after the opening of the railway, and rather distorts the proportions of the Rocket-type engine. Subsequent quadrupling has scarcely lessened the grandeur of this excavation.

The deviation of route on the approach to Liverpool meant crossing the valley of the Sankey Brook further downstream than originally intended, and the consequent building of the Sankey viaduct, with its nine arches each of fifty foot span, at a cost of £45,000. In the foreground of this familiar Ackermann print it crosses the pioneer Sankey Brook Navigation, a canal authorised in 1755 and completed soon afterwards.

Opponents of the Liverpool & Manchester saw the undrained peat mass of Chat Moss as a formidable obstacle to the building of the railway, and estimated the cost of its crossing as high as £270,000. In the event, little more than one-tenth of this sum was needed. Shaw's engraving captures the lonely and desolate atmosphere of the vast expanse of fen, an atmosphere that subsequent reclamation has not entirely dispelled.

From Edge Hill, tunnels were necessary to reach both the passenger terminus at Crown Street and the goods warehouse adjacent to the docks at Wapping. C. & G. Pyne's engraving shows construction under way at Edge Hill.

Ackermann's print of the Wapping tunnel is inaccurate, both in the apparent size of the tunnel in relation to the human figures and in the depiction of steam traction. In subsequent editions, the locomotive was removed—at first by the simple expedient of erasing its chimney—and the cable added. The gas jets which initially lit the tunnel are prominent.

Crown Street was closed to passenger traffic after the opening of Lime Street in 1836. The restricted proportions of the original single track approach tunnel are shown in the photograph taken about 1925, with horse haulage of wagons to the coal yard.

The approach to Wapping was through a tunnel 1 mile 351 yd long on a gradient of 1 in 48. This Ackermann print shows the warehouse at Wapping, and the tunnel mouth with the cable for haulage.

Park Lane goods station, as Wapping was subsequently known, was closed on 1 November 1965. In this view, taken in January 1966, it is still intact with its graceful iron pillars and massive crane. The tunnel mouth can be seen in the background.

Cable haulage through the Wapping tunnel lasted until 11 May 1896. One of the wagons formerly used in the haulage of trains is seen here, with the grip for attaching it to the cable visible on the right. The right hand figure is Samuel Strong, Foreman.

THE ROUTE NORTH

There were few physical obstacles south from industrial Lancashire. A link with the Midlands was completed by the opening of the Grand Junction Railway from Warrington to Birmingham on 4 July 1837; the country it traversed was so easy that the cost of construction was only £18,846 per mile. The route to the north was a very different proposition. As far as Lancaster there were few problems but beyond lay the formidable upland barrier of the Lake District and Shap Fell.

For a time, the barrier was circumvented by a combination of rail and sea transport. The Preston & Wyre Railway was opened to Fleetwood on 16 July 1840; from May 1841 passengers could travel by rail to Fleetwood, from there by the steamship **Fire King** to Ardrossan and then by rail again to Glasgow. As the *Railway Times* remarked, 'What more can any reasonable man want? If he were to travel the whole way by rail at the rate of 20 miles an hour, he could but arrive two or three hours earlier, before breakfast was ready or anyone up to bid him welcome.' At Fleetwood, travellers were greeted by the beginnings of the new town founded by Sir Peter Hesketh-Fleetwood in 1836, and laid out by Decimus Burton. Almost opposite the station lay the North Euston Hotel, its pillared portico a reflection, albeit in a minor key, of Euston's Doric arch. The photograph also shows the lighthouse on the edge of the shore, another of Burton's classical-featured buildings.

Several canal companies in the North West reacted in a very positive way to the railway challenge. Some promoted railways themselves. In 1831, the Manchester, Bolton & Bury Canal sought to convert their navigation into a railway, but in the event were content to build a line alongside the canal. The railway, opened on 29 May 1838, is here seen beside the now-derelict canal at Pendleton. Pendleton Station was closed on 5 December 1966 and the buildings are here being demolished in September 1967.

North of Preston, a canal company took over an existing railway. The Lancaster & Preston Junction Railway, opened on 25 June 1840, suffered from lack of a rail outlet north of Lancaster and from competition from the closely parallel Lancaster Canal. Its plight became such that it was leased for a period by the canal company from 1 September 1842. Here Class 5 44848 heads a Wolverhampton-Stirling train through the gentle country north of Preston. The Lancaster Canal is in the foreground.

North of Lancaster, schemes for a railway over the fells to Carlisle and Scotland date back to the mid-1830s. In 1839, a Commission was appointed to consider the merits of various proposals, which by then had crystallised into three main schemes. The advantages of a coastal route, with easy gradients compensating for increased mileage, had been propounded by George Stephenson in 1837, but his relatively modest ideas for embankments across the head of Morecambe Bay were superseded by John Hague's over-ambitious scheme for a direct embankment more than ten miles long. Inland, two routes were canvassed, both with fairly long summit tunnels and sustained gradients of 1 in 140. One followed the Lune valley, and tunnelled under Orton Scar, the other passed through the important town of Kendal, but needed a longer tunnel to reach Haweswater and Penrith.

The Commissioners recommended an inland route, but felt that an alignment could be found which served Kendal yet used the physical advantages of the upper Lune valley. In the event, the engineer of the Lancaster & Carlisle, Joseph Locke, followed the general line suggested by this compromise but avoided a tunnel completely by climbing over Shap Fell with a gradient of four miles of unbroken 1 in 75. The Lancaster & Carlisle was opened throughout on 15 December 1846, a date recalled by the bridge over the Sedbergh road near Oxenholme until its recent replacement during the laying of continuous-welded track. The photograph was taken in 1963.

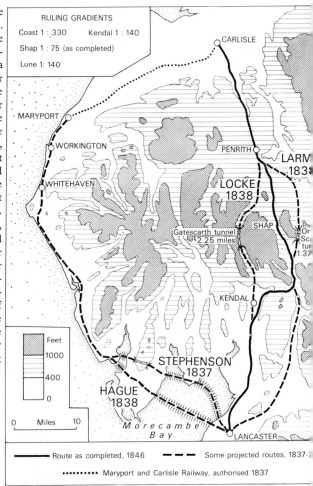

RULING GRADIENTS

Coast 1 : 330   Kendal 1 : 140

Shap 1 : 75 (as completed)

Lune 1 : 140

——————— Route as completed, 1846   – – – – Some projected routes, 1837–

•••••••• Maryport and Carlisle Railway, authorised 1837

One of the most impressive engineering features of the Lancaster & Carlisle was the bridge across the Lune immediately north of Lancaster Castle Station, carrying the railway fifty-five feet above the tidal river. As built (top), the seven short stone spans on the south bank, on the right, were succeeded by three 120 ft spans, each made of layers of timber planks fastened together by wooden pins and strengthened by rods and bands of iron. The photograph was taken not long before its rebuilding only twenty years after construction. In the foreground is the then single-track line of the 'little' North Western Railway between Lancaster and Morecambe, opened on 12 June 1848, and ultimately doubled in 1877.

On rebuilding, the laminated timber arches were replaced by wrought iron girders which remained until a further rebuilding almost a century later in 1962-3. In the centre photograph, taken on 26 October 1962, the second reconstruction is in progress, while the completed spans, in reinforced concrete, are seen below. The springing for the original timber arches on the stone piers can still be discerned.

After the climb from Oxenholme to Grayrigg, the Lancaster & Carlisle swings into the Lune Gorge at Low Gill. Here, at Dillicar, a north-bound freight runs alongside the river while beyond tower the Howgills, rising to over 2,000 ft.

North of Tebay, the line climbs out of the valley on to the fells at Shap Summit, 916 ft above sea-level. The open moorland of the watershed is clearly evident in these views, at the favourite photographer's viewpoint just short of the summit cutting. At the turn of the century (top) a Webb 'Jumbo' heads an Aberdeen express, one of the LNWR postcards of 1905. On 18 June 1928 (centre) 'Royal Scot' 6108 **Seaforth Highlander**, less than a year old, is seen on the 'Royal Scot'. On 9 July 1963 (bottom) rebuilt 'Royal Scot' 46160 **Queen Victoria's Rifleman**, with less than two years active existence remaining, pilots rebuilt 'Patriot' 45512 **Bunsen** on an eighteen-coach empty stock train.

ABERDEEN EXPRESS ON SHAP SUMMIT.

ROUTES EAST

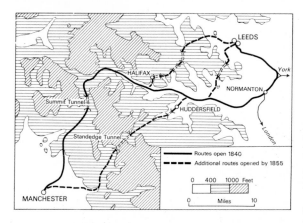

Eastwards, the Pennines offered another formidable barrier to the railway builders. Nevertheless, the prospect of traffic between the industrial areas of Lancashire and Yorkshire proved a powerful incentive to early construction. The first line across was the Manchester & Leeds, opened to Littleborough on 4 July 1839, and completed throughout to Normanton on 1 March 1841. With a choice of routes available, the company's engineer George Stephenson characteristically tried to keep the gradients as easy as possible, even at the expense of great mileage (above). By adopting a circuitous route through Rochdale, the Pennine watershed could be crossed at a height of less than 600 ft, utilising the approaches to a through valley at Littleborough cut by meltwater in glacial times. As a result, the gradients are the least and the tunnels the shortest of any of the trans-Pennine routes out of Manchester.

The engraving, from Smiles' biography of Stephenson, depicts the southern approaches to the summit gorge. The Rochdale Canal has climbed high enough to pass through the gorge without a tunnel, though at the expense of ninety-two locks between Manchester and Sowerby Bridge.

The southern portal of Summit tunnel, with Class 8F 2—8—0 48639 heading towards Rochdale with an express freight. Though the shortest of the trans-Pennine tunnels, it was still a formidable work. 1 mile 1,125 yd long, it took three years to bore and cost £300,000. Fourteen shafts were used to assist excavation, the deepest 341 ft from the top to rail level.

A more direct route across the Pennines between Manchester and Mirfield was provided by the opening on 1 August 1849 of the line between Stalybridge and Huddersfield. This utilised the valley of the Tame to approach the watershed, but the gain in mileage was at the expense of steeper gradients and a summit tunnel 3 miles 62 yd long.

This line is another example of a railway promoted by a canal company, and in consequence it runs parallel to, though at times some little distance from, the Huddersfield Narrow Canal. At Standedge, the existing canal tunnel was used to carry spoil away from the headings of the adjoining railway bore, the initial single-track tunnel being a little higher and fifty feet to the south. At Diggle (below) a westbound 'Trans-Pennine' diesel multiple-unit, strengthened at the leading end by a two-car Derby unit, has just left the double track Standedge North tunnel completed in 1894: in the foreground is the entrance to the canal tunnel, now abandoned for navigation.

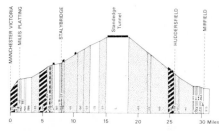

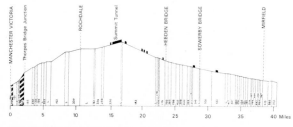

LONDON AND NORTH WESTERN RAILWAY, 1849

MANCHESTER AND LEEDS RAILWAY, 1840

The physical problems of railway building in the valleys of the Pennines are exemplified by this view of Saddleworth viaduct, here being crossed on a crisp February day in 1967 by Class 4MT 75035 with an eastbound freight climbing to Standedge.

The Sheffield, Ashton-under-Lyne & Manchester Railway followed the valley of the Etherow to approach its summit tunnel at Woodhead. The alignment surveyed by Charles Vignoles necessitated gradients as steep as 1 in 100, very severe for a line authorised in 1837 though not opened throughout until 22 December 1845. Dinting Vale was spanned by five laminated timber arches, each 125 ft in span: together with the approach arches, the viaduct had a total length of 1,452 ft, and a height above Glossop Brook of 125 ft. It was designed by the SA & M's Resident Engineer, A. S. Jee: part of his original drawings are reproduced (right). As with the Lune viaduct at Lancaster, the timber arches at Dinting had a relatively short life and

were replaced by wrought iron girders in 1860. Further strengthening later became necessary, and in 1918-19 seven extra piers were added. This strengthening cost £41,600, compared with the total cost of the original viaduct in 1844 of £35,250. Visually, the additional piers ruined the appearance of the viaduct, as this 1967 photograph (top) with an eastbound train of coal empties, clearly shows.

The wild country at the head of the climb towards Woodhead, looking down the Longdendale valley from over the mouth of the new Woodhead tunnel, with a Manchester-Sheffield express approaching on 8 September 1966. Electrification of the former Sheffield, Ashton-under-Lyne & Manchester route was completed in 1954, though the scheme was initiated by the LNER in 1935. It was the first trunk freight route to be converted to electric traction, a conversion undertaken because of the difficulties of working heavy coal traffic over its steep gradients.

MANIA & AFTERMATH

The flurry of speculative railway promotion between 1844 and 1846 left its mark in the North West. By the mid-1840s, north-south and east-west trunk routes were complete or under construction, but as yet the density of railways even in south Lancashire was not great and no directly competing lines had been built. During the Railway Mania of 1845-6, the fever of promotion led to a rash of schemes; the map shows only those actually authorised by Parliament, but they included such proposals as new trunk routes across the northern Pennines as well as many more firmly rooted in commercial good sense. By 1852, completed railway mileage had expanded dramatically, but the desolate uplands north of Skipton remained devoid of railways despite earlier authorisations. To the south, however, a much denser network was now in operation in industrial Lancashire.

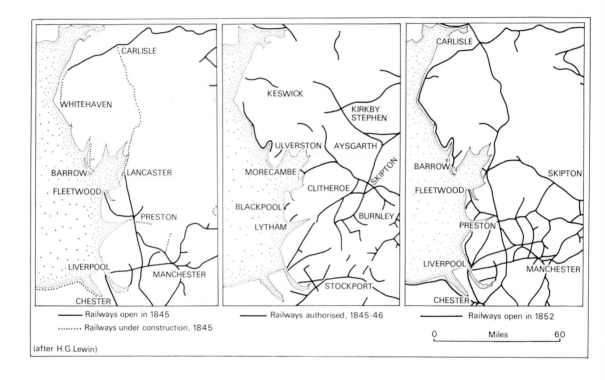

Railways open in 1845
.... Railways under construction, 1845

Railways authorised, 1845-46

Railways open in 1852

0   Miles   60

(after H.G.Lewin)

A monument to Mania speculation, the Fleetwood, Preston & West Riding Junction Railway was authorised in 1846 to build sixteen miles of railway to the north of the Ribble between Longridge and Clitheroe, as part of an attempt to channel West Riding traffic to the port of Fleetwood. Work began at Hurst Green, but was quickly suspended when another company failed to begin work on its section east of Clitheroe. This cutting at Hurst Green remains as a tangible but isolated witness to the scheme; it has never carried rails and is still more than three miles from the nearest railway.

The increasing proliferation of railways brought competition and even active hostility between companies. At Clifton Junction, west of Manchester, the existing Lancashire & Yorkshire route was joined on 28 September 1846 by the East Lancashire line from Bury: tolls payable by the ELR for the use of LYR metals to Salford became a major bone of contention and led to the 'battle' of Clifton Junction on 12 March 1849 (above). Passage from the East Lancashire line, swinging in from the right background, is blocked by the LYR train on the right: in retaliation, the ELR have placed a train of stone-laden wagons on the other line. Eight trains were ultimately jammed round the junction before the blockading LYR train was moved. In 1964 (right) the ELR signal box has long been replaced by a standard LYR box on the other side of the tracks. The ELR was absorbed by the LYR in 1859.

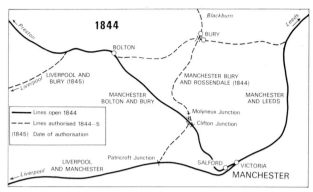

1844

Blackburn

BURY

BOLTON

Preston

Leeds

Liverpool

LIVERPOOL AND
BURY (1845)

MANCHESTER BURY
AND ROSSENDALE (1844)

MANCHESTER
BOLTON AND BURY

MANCHESTER
AND LEEDS

Molyneux Junction

Clifton Junction

— Lines open 1844
- - - Lines authorised 1844—5
(1845) Date of authorisation

Patricroft Junction

LIVERPOOL
AND MANCHESTER

SALFORD   VICTORIA

Liverpool

MANCHESTER

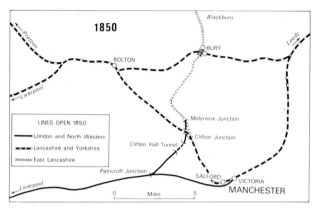

1850

Blackburn

BURY

BOLTON

Preston

Leeds

Liverpool

Molyneux Junction

Clifton Junction

Clifton Hall Tunnel

LINES OPEN 1850
—— London and North Western
-=-=- Lancashire and Yorkshire
······· East Lancashire

Patricroft Junction

SALFORD   VICTORIA

Liverpool

MANCHESTER

0   Miles   5

Rapidly changing company alliances made some lines redundant almost before they were opened. The line from Patricroft Junction to Molyneux Junction was promoted by the Liverpool & Manchester to carry Liverpool-Bury traffic when its monopoly east of Liverpool was threatened by the promotion of the Liverpool & Bury in 1845 (upper map). By the time these lines were completed, company allegiances (and company titles) had changed (lower map). The LNWR and the LYR coexisted in comparative harmony, but relations between them and the East Lancashire were strained. In these circumstances, the Patricroft Junction-Molyneux Junction line lost its principal justification, and passenger services were withdrawn only three months after they were instituted in February 1850.

The line survived for goods traffic until April 1953, when Clifton Hall tunnel collapsed, involving several houses above it and causing a number of deaths. The abandoned southern approaches to the tunnel are seen (below) a decade after the closure.

At Clifton Junction station further remnants of the line from Patricroft Junction are evident. The rusting metals pass under the former LYR line (right) and rise to join the former East Lancashire line (below) at Molyneux Junction itself, in the background beyond the station platforms.

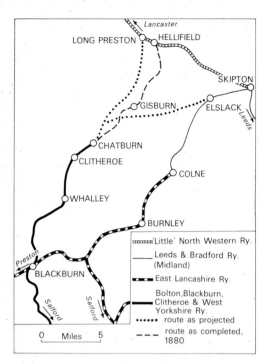

The fluctuating fortunes of some lines promoted during the Mania are exemplified by that between Blackburn and Hellifield. It was conceived as a link between lines in the Manchester area and the envisaged routes of the 'little' North Western and Leeds & Bradford Railways for traffic to Scotland via Ingleton and to the industrial West Riding respectively (map). It was authorised in 1846 as the Blackburn, Clitheroe & North Western; when the Mania 'bubble' burst, with its aftermath of depression and financial troubles, it amalgamated in 1847 with the line to Bolton as the Bolton, Blackburn, Clitheroe & North Western Junction, hoping thereby to ease financial stress and speed construction. In the event, it was not until the summer of 1850 that it was complete as far as Chatburn where it was terminated until times were more propitious.

This first section was boldly laid out. Whalley viaduct (below) straddled the Calder valley, its long succession of arches making a powerful effect by their repeated rhythm, 'stretching away in a countless series into the distance' in Jack Simmons' description. It is here being crossed on 8 October 1967 by a Sunday Crewe-Carlisle parcels train, diverted from the main West Coast route.

Completion of the route beyond Chatburn was delayed for thirty years, until the Midland was building its new main line north from Settle to Carlisle. The provision of a link to feed Lancashire traffic into the new route had obvious commercial attractions, and a line from Chatburn to Hellifield was opened on 1 June 1880, with a rather different alignment from that initially envisaged. North of Gisburn (above) it twists sinuously through the rolling 'drumlin' terrain, thereby keeping earthworks and consequent construction costs to a minimum. It remains an important through link: here Class 9F 92218 heads a southbound train of anhydrite from Long Meg sidings near Lazonby in the Eden valley.

At Gisburn, a 156 yd tunnel was built in fulfilment of a clause in the authorising Act requiring the construction of a covered way beneath Gisburn Park to preserve the amenities of the estate. The extremely shallow cover of the tunnel, and its ornamental design are clearly evident.

RURAL RAILWAYS

In the second half of the nineteenth century the railway network expanded to serve territory hitherto remote from its benefits. Rural areas, though with only slender traffic prospects, were tapped both by branches of existing main line railways and by independent companies. The stopping passenger and the pick-up goods became the symbol of the railway as the universal carrier; it is scarcely surprising that many such services succumbed early to road competition.

On the borders of Dumfriesshire and Cumberland, J39 64884 brings a Langholm-Carlisle local into Canonbie. This picture sums up much of the rural line; the well-tended single platform station with its simple buildings, the small knot of passengers, the oil lamps and the crate of milk. Passenger services were withdrawn from this former North British branch from 15 June 1964.

Half a century earlier, in 1907, Furness Railway 2—4—2 tank 72, rebuilt in 1890 from a 2—4—0 tender engine, pauses (right) at Greenodd station on the Windermere Lakeside branch. Passenger trains finally ceased to call here from 30 September 1946, though services had been sporadic for several years.

The rural setting of Hesketh Bank Station (below) on the erstwhile West Lancashire Railway between Southport and Preston is strikingly obvious, open fields coming right to the edge of the station. The Preston-bound train is hauled by Class 4MT 75047 shortly before all services were withdrawn on 7 September 1964.

In the Lake District, tourist prospects heightened the area's appeal to the railway promoter, though the only line to cross the region was the Cockermouth, Keswick & Penrith, opened on 2 January 1865. In leafy surroundings, Ivatt Class 2MT 46433 rolls into Keswick with a Penrith-Workington train, the fireman handing over the token for the single line section which the train has left (below).

The CK & P was closed west of Keswick from 18 April 1966: in August 1964, a Keswick-bound diesel multiple-unit from Whitehaven nears its destination with Grisedale Pike, 2,593 ft, dominating the skyline (above).

The southern Lake District was Furness Railway terrain. The Coniston branch, opened on 18 June 1859, lasted until 30 April 1962: at Coniston (top), with its characteristic overall roof, Ivatt Class 2MT 41217 stands with the Foxfield Junction train shortly before the withdrawal of passenger services in 1958. On Windermere, steamer services are still popular. **Swan** (centre) is given a coat of paint high and dry on the slip at Lakeside. Lakeside station (below) was opened on 1 June 1869 with commodious facilities for rail and steamer passengers, but rail services ceased from 6 September 1965.

URBAN & SUBURBAN

As the conurbations of Manchester and Merseyside grew in size, railway services handled a growing volume of commuter traffic. Most was carried on previously existing routes, but some lines were built specially to cater for it. Electrification later enabled selected lines to operate intensive services more effectively.

The Lancashire & Yorkshire was a pioneer of suburban electrification. North of Manchester, its Irk valley route to Bury, opened on 1 September 1879 to serve the expanding suburbs of Prestwich and White-field, was electrified in 1916 at 1,200V DC third-rail contact. The Horwich-built all-steel rolling stock for this service was long-lived:

a five-car train is seen at Radcliffe Central (above) shortly before its withdrawal in 1959. A four-car train of the replacement stock (below) approaches Queens Road Junction soon after leaving Manchester Victoria.

Glossop (above) is now the terminal for a suburban electric service over the former Great Central route to Manchester. The branch from the main line at Dinting was originally built as a private line in 1845 by the Duke of Norfolk. It was electrified at 1,500V DC in 1954 as part of the Manchester-Sheffield scheme.

South of Manchester, the Altrincham line had its genesis in a scheme to convert the Bridgewater Canal into a railway from Manchester to Runcorn. It was opened to Altrincham as part of the joint Manchester, South Junction & Altrincham Railway on 1 August 1849, not replacing the canal but running alongside it for much of its route, as seen here (below) on the approaches to Dane Road. It was electrified at 1,500V DC in 1931. Until 1963, four tracks were provided at this point, but the two nearest the canal have now been lifted.

On Merseyside, urban and suburban traffic stimulated the building of three independent railways as well as the development of suburban services by main-line companies. Tunnelling under the Mersey with gradients as steep as 1 in 27, the Mersey Railway was opened on 1 February 1886. Prior to electrification in 1903 (the first such conversion in Britain), powerful steam locomotives were essential: one of these, Beyer Peacock 0—6—4T **Cecil Raikes**, has survived after a period of service at Ilkeston Colliery, and on 2 March 1965 (top) was handed over to Liverpool City Museum for restoration and eventual display.

On Wirral, services to New Brighton and West Kirby were provided by the Wirral Railway of which the first section was opened on 2 July 1866. No 14, built by Beyer Peacock in 1903 with the unusual 4—4—4T wheel arrangement, rounds the curve into Birkenhead North about 1920 (centre).

The Wirral lines were electrified by the LMS in 1938, trains then working through to Liverpool over the Mersey Railway. In BR days, a six-car train of LMS-pattern stock leaves New Brighton for Liverpool Central (bottom).

Passenger movement along the line of Liverpool's docks was catered for by the Liverpool Overhead Railway, opened on 6 March 1893, the first overhead electric railway in the world, and the first line in Britain to be equipped with automatic signalling. During construction, the spans were assembled at the north end of the line, transported by trolley over the finished portion of the structure, and finally placed in position (above) by the 'Ives Patent Gantry'.

A two-car LOR train heads south from James Street Station about 1908 (below). Immediately above the leading car can be seen the Mersey Railway's Georges Dock Pumping Station, and to the left, on Pier Head, the then new Dock Offices, completed in 1907. Horse-drawn drays crowd the Strand (the original shore-line of the Mersey). Services on the LOR ceased on 30 December 1956, renewal of the decking being too costly for the company to undertake.

The coastal resorts of Lancashire and North Wales became attractive residential areas for the more affluent commuters of Manchester and Merseyside. Particularly in the case of Manchester, traffic was encouraged by the provision of express services with the commuter in mind. On Christmas Eve 1964, Class 5 45278 waits at Southport Chapel Street with the 7.55 am to Manchester (above).

Manchester's merchant princes were not satisfied with first class alone for their journey to work. In spacious Edwardian days, the LYR and the LNWR ran special saloon coaches, to which none but members of a club were admitted, on services between Manchester and Blackpool, Windermere and Llandudno. The LMS continued the tradition: the exterior and interior of Club Car 822 built in 1935 for the Blackpool service (right).

EXPANDING FACILITIES

As traffic grew in the railway age, existing facilities were expanded to cater for it, with bigger stations, duplicate running lines, more sidings for storage and marshalling and improvements to existing routes.

Victoria station, Manchester, was claimed to be the biggest in England at the time of its opening on 1 January 1844, yet as Tait's 1845 lithograph shows, all traffic in both Liverpool and Leeds directions was handled at a single platform though four other storage tracks ran under the graceful iron roof. Such a situation did not long suffice; Victoria saw successive rebuildings in 1864, 1884 and 1904, while further relief was given by the removal of LNWR traffic to the adjacent Exchange station, opened in 1884 and effectively a part of Victoria in all but name. Victoria today has seventeen platform faces (below): uppermost are the ten terminal platforms and the through platform 11 (which continues to Exchange), while on the near side of the station are the remaining five through platforms.

Duplicate running lines at key points avoid conflicting movements. Immediately north of Carlisle, relief goods lines were provided in 1877 between Willowholme and Caldew Junctions. The photograph (left) probably dates from September 1877, and work is being completed on the laying of tracks over the new bridge spanning the River Caldew. North of the bridge, the North British route swings away from the Caledonian main line: the Caledonian's Port Carlisle Junction signal box can be seen, this being replaced later by Carlisle No 3. The signals, surprisingly, appear to be of LNWR Saxby & Farmer type.

Over eighty years later, 'Duchess' 46222 **Queen Mary** heads the northbound 'Royal Scot' out of Carlisle over the River Eden (below). Immediately above the rear coaches is Port Carlisle Junction and beyond the bridges over the Caldew can just be discerned. In the right foreground are relief lines built during the second world war.

One of the major schemes carried out between the wars by the LNER was the building of Mottram yard on the Manchester-Sheffield line, work being completed in 1935. During construction of the yard, an unidentified D 11/1 'Director' passes Gamesley with a Sheffield express. The yard control tower, showing just above the engine's cab, is also prominent in the foreground of the lower picture, which shows the sorting sidings in 1966. A six-car electric multiple-unit on the Glossop-Manchester Piccadilly local service is passing on the main line.

Physical difficulties deterred a crossing of the Mersey below Warrington until 1863, when work began on a bridge at Runcorn Gap, where the river channel narrows. The completed viaduct, with three main lattice girder spans each 305 ft long and 75 ft above high water level, was opened on 1 February 1869. In 1961, the new road bridge nears completion, to supersede the transporter bridge of 1905.

Until the 1860s the original Liverpool & Manchester route from Lime Street carried not only Manchester traffic but that for London and the north as well: in addition, between Newton Junction at Earlestown and West Junction at Parkside it formed part of the West Coast main line (right). The opening of a series of cut-offs both shortened journeys and reduced congestion. The Winwick Junction-Golborne Junction line was opened on 1 August 1864; at Winwick Junction (below) Class 5 44677 passes with a southbound freight on the direct main-line, while Class 4MT 76075 with another freight waits for a path from the earlier route from Earlestown. In the background is the Vulcan Foundry, founded as a locomotive building works by Robert Stephenson and Charles Tayleur in 1832, and now incorporated into the English Electric group.

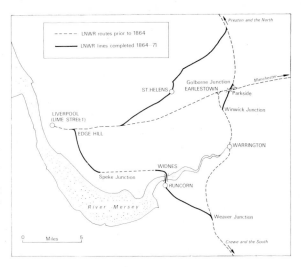

MIDLAND TO MANCHESTER & THE MERSEY

The railway network was intensified by the penetration of lines built by companies with no previous stake in the area. The Midland, an erstwhile provincial company centred on Derby, underwent a period of rapid expansion from the late 1850s, creating a new main line from London to the north. So far as Lancashire was concerned, the nearest point on its system lay beyond the Pennines to the south-east, but in 1861 it came to an agreement with the Manchester, Sheffield & Lincolnshire to extend its own route to New Mills and from there run over the latter company's metals to London Road. The resulting line, though direct, crossed difficult country. The Pennine watershed was crossed at a height of 980 ft at Peak Forest with long stretches on each side at the ruling gradient of 1 in 90 and with major tunnels and viaducts. Through passenger service from Manchester to London over the Midland route began on 1 February 1867.

The scenery of the Derbyshire Peak is truly magnificent. The up 'Midland Pullman' runs along Chee Dale in the hazy sunlight of a July morning in 1965. The train itself was a brief reminder of the former glories of the Midland route; with first-class Pullman accommodation only, it provided the fastest service between Manchester and London —in 3 h 10 m—from its introduction in 1960 until its withdrawal in 1966 on completion of the electrification of the Manchester-Crewe-Euston line.

Now after just over a century trains are to cease to run altogether through this part of the Peak, through services being diverted to the Hope Valley route. The spirit of Ruskin at least will be delighted, for he fought bitterly to preserve the valley of the Wye from the railway's 'close-clinging damnation'.

Still in the valley of the Wye, but some four miles to the south-east, just south of Monsal Dale station, 'Jubilee' 45689 **Ajax** heads an up express in the mid-1950s.

The permanent Manchester terminus of the Cheshire Lines Committee, Manchester Central, was opened on 1 July 1880. Midland influence in its design is evident; the great span of its roof is similar to that of St Pancras, though its span of 210 ft is 30 ft shorter than its London counterpart. It was built by a Derby firm, even though a local company had tendered a lower bid. Type 4 diesel D38 has just arrived with a St Pancras train on 30 December 1966.

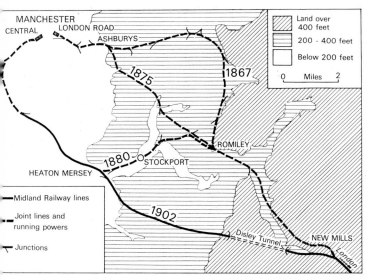

Midland expresses followed four different routes into Manchester within thirty-five years (top). At first they shared the cramped MS & L accommodation at London Road, improving the indirect approach through Hyde by building a direct line from Romiley to Ashburys. From 1 August 1880, they were routed over CLC lines into the valley of the Mersey at Stockport and the new South District line to Cornbrook Junction and Central. This was a busy and devious approach with numerous junctions; on 1 July 1902 an independent, direct route from New Mills to Heaton Mersey was opened to passenger traffic.

In its directness, this line showed a considerable disregard for relief and was in consequence expensive to build. Forsaking the valley of the Goyt at New Mills, it pierced the ridge between the Goyt and the Mersey by Disley tunnel, at 2 miles 346 yd the sixth longest in Britain. Class 8F 48528 enters Disley tunnel with an up freight in 1955 (centre).

As Disley was being built, one of the tunnels on the original line, Bugsworth, was opened up to form a cutting. The last section was demolished on Sunday 10 August 1902 (bottom).

59

In extending its influence west of Manchester, the Midland joined forces with the MS & L and the Great Northern, becoming a partner in the Cheshire Lines Committee in 1866. The initials of the component companies of the CLC are still carved on the facade of Stockport Tiviot Dale station (right), a handsome brick building with an arcaded frontage (left). The CLC's direct route from Manchester to Liverpool was opened on 1 March 1873; after the opening of Manchester Central, an express service was established between the two cities, taking forty-five minutes for the thirty-four miles. Motive power was provided by the MS & L —in later Great Central days, the last batch of Pollitt singles, built in 1900, were frequent performers and 971, her Pollitt stovepipe replaced by a shapely Robinson chimney, heads one of the expresses shortly before grouping (bottom).

At Liverpool, the initial CLC terminus at Brunswick, opened 1 June 1864, was well to the south-east of the city centre and naturally failed to attract much traffic even though passengers and their luggage were carried free by omnibus to and from James Street near the Town Hall. As in the case of the Liverpool & Manchester over thirty years earlier, an extension was obviously necessary; on 1 March 1874 a new line, largely in tunnel, was opened from Brunswick to a terminus on Ranelagh Street. Liverpool Central also had a single span overall roof, but it was neither as wide nor as steeply pitched as its Manchester counterpart.

MIDLAND FOR SCOTLAND

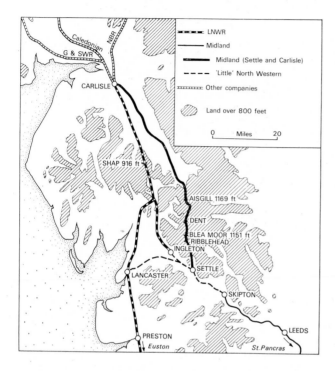

Map legend:
- LNWR
- Midland
- Midland (Settle and Carlisle)
- 'Little' North Western
- Other companies
- Land over 800 feet

0 Miles 20

Having conquered the Pennines to Manchester, the Midland sought to be an Anglo-Scottish carrier in its own right. Tiring of ineffectual connections and interminable delays with the LNWR at Ingleton, the company promoted an independent route from Settle to Carlisle. Opened eventually for freight on 2 August 1875, and for passenger traffic nine months later, the line achieved independence but at a high price. It cost three and a half million pounds for the seventy-two miles of route, and in crossing from the headwaters of the Ribble to those of the Eden it runs continuously above one thousand feet for over seventeen miles, never far from the main Pennine watershed.

In Midland days, one class of locomotive came to be particularly associated with the Settle & Carlisle, Deeley's 999 Class 4—4—0s, of which ten were built between 1907 and 1909, spending virtually all their working lives north of Leeds. In many ways, they were a simple version of the contemporary Compounds. 992 is seen at Armathwaite about 1912, at the head of a nine-coach express of Clayton and Bain clerestorey stock.

Tunnel and viaduct come in swift succession as the line clings to its chosen path high up towards the watershed. Blea Moor tunnel (right) is the longest at 2,629 yd. At the southern end (seen here with a Type 4 'Peak' class diesel emerging with the up 'Thames-Clyde Express' in April 1967) it was originally intended to extend the approach cutting 400 yd further into the fell side, but the danger of slips led to tunnelling instead. This first section of the tunnel lies on a curve: its alignment can be traced by the spoil heaps and ventilation shaft on the moor beyond.

Arten Gill viaduct carries the line across one of the numerous tributary streams tumbling into Dentdale (below). Its eleven spans total 220 yd in length, the highest 117 ft above the beck, though it was necessary to sink the piers a further 55 ft beneath the surface to get a secure foundation. It is built of local stone, Dent Marble, a dark grey to black limestone with fossils standing out in sharp white contrast. A Class 9F 2—10—0 crosses with a southbound train of anhydrite from Long Meg sidings in August 1967.

Ribblehead viaduct, longest and loftiest on the Settle & Carlisle, is crossed by a Type 2 diesel with a northbound freight. Completed in 1875, the viaduct is 440 yd long and 165 ft high, its twenty-four spans built of local Great Scar limestone from the quarry between Selside and Ribblehead.

A MIDLAND TRAIN SNOWED UP, NEAR DENT.

Its sustained height and exposure have long made the Settle & Carlisle susceptible to the vagaries of weather, and tales of the battle with the elements reach legendary proportions. Snow is a particular hazard and conditions do not change with the years. The caption to F. S. Williams' engraving of the 1880s (above) would serve equally well for the scene below of a Type 4 'Peak' class diesel marooned with its train on the bleak stretch of line between Rise Hill tunnel and Dent station during a blizzard in January 1963.

E

Nearing the summit of the 'Long Drag', the gruelling fourteen and a half miles of almost continuous 1 in 100 from Settle Junction up to Blea Moor. In the background, the flat-topped summit of Ingleborough rises to 2,373 ft; the railway itself is over 1,100 ft high at this point.

CONURBATION CONTRASTS

Merseyside and Manchester both have an intensive, complex railway network. But there the similarity largely ends. Most traffic into Merseyside, with its coastal location, is of a terminal nature, and the various approach routes have remained largely independent. In Manchester, through traffic has a much more important part to play and a complicated network of linking lines, often jointly owned, has resulted.

In Liverpool, the sandstone ridge parallel to the Mersey makes rail access to the city centre difficult from the east. Nevertheless, this approach was adopted by the Liverpool & Manchester Railway; in consequence, its 1836 extension from Edge Hill to Lime Street has to drop steeply to the terminus on a gradient of 1 in 93. The line was originally in tunnel, but this was opened up when the tracks were quadrupled in 1881. Cable haulage was used initially, but abandoned in March 1870. The stability of the sandstone enabled the walls of the deep cutting to be vertical and largely without brick facing. In this 1963 view, the platforms at Lime Street are immediately beyond the cutting with its succession of overbridges. Motive power is in transition, with electric haulage of trains, but station shunting still performed by Class 3F steam tank engines—in this instance 47357.

The heart of Liverpool is ringed by its passenger terminals, but their approaches are not linked. This air view looks north-west across the city centre to the Mersey, with New Brighton on the far shore. On the lower left is Central's single span roof, the approach tracks plunging into tunnel at the station throat. Above, and rather hidden by cloud shadow, is Exchange, whose approaches run astride their viaduct just inland from the line of the docks and almost parallel with the top of the picture. On the right are Lime Street's massive curved spans, looking across the street whose name they bear to the classical grandeur of St George's Hall, completed in 1854. Railway hotels also add their contribution to the scene. They form the frontage of both Exchange and Lime Street, though the latter's North Western Hotel was converted to offices and is now to be demolished. The Midland's Adelphi stands in relative isolation midway between Central and Lime Street, a splendid caravanserai.

Liverpool's passenger terminals now closely adjoin the business and commercial heart of the city, even if they do not actually penetrate it, but each is a replacement of an earlier structure sited further out (map). The benefits of a more convenient location had to be balanced against the high cost of land acquisition towards the central area and of the engineering works involved, but increasing traffic justified such expenditure. Even so, the new sites were relatively restricted in area and handled only passenger terminal traffic, with minimum storage and servicing facilities. The earlier stations became goods depots, a function still retained by Crown Street and Brunswick. Brunswick lasted longest as a passenger station; the original building still survives (below), though swamped in scale by the adjacent goods warehouse, boldly blazoned with the names of the constituent companies of the CLC.

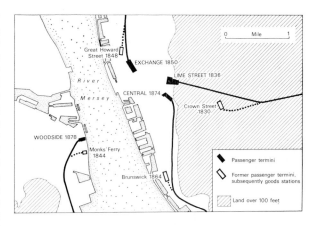

As in Liverpool, the high-rising buildings of Manchester's commercial heart are closely ringed by railway stations, but the very different nature of traffic flows has led to the establishment of an almost complete encircling belt of connecting lines, carried high on viaducts to avoid incessant street crossings at ground level. The initial pattern was simple—five lines radiating from four unconnected terminals (opposite)—but the lack of interchange facilities soon created problems and it was to their mutual advantage for companies to promote linking lines, often jointly owned. Within seven years in the 1840s a complete system of links had been created; for traffic to west, north and east, a single through station, Victoria, had replaced the earlier terminals at Liverpool Road and Oldham Road, Salford also becoming a through station. Later additions to the railway network were refinements to improve working, often stimulated by competition. Congestion at Victoria was relieved by duplicate approach lines and by the building of Exchange, the CLC created its independent approach to Central, and individual companies established separate freight facilities as with the Midland at Ancoats, and the Great Northern at Deansgate. The plethora of duplicate facilities is a problem for contemporary rationalisation—and an even greater problem for the innocent traveller.

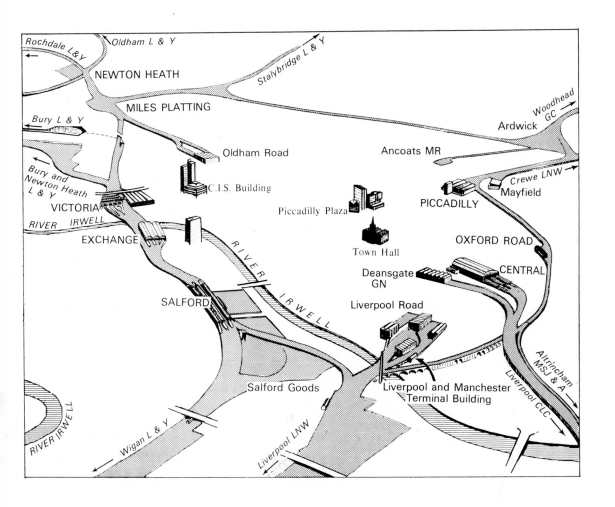

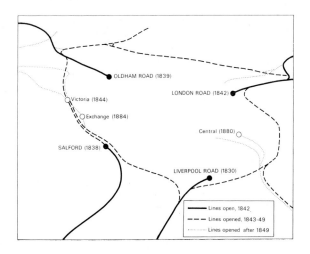

RAILWAY STRUCTURES

Railway structures, by their number and variety, create a distinctive landscape of their own. Some are individual buildings of distinction, others examples of standardised design, but together they give to each line a peculiar savour, and one which alters but little with the years despite changing railway ownership and changing railway trains.

Francis Thompson's long and elegant facade at Chester General is still virtually the same as when J. Romney's engraving was published in 1853. Chester General, opened on 1 August 1848, was a classic example of the 'one-sided' station with but one through platform for both up and down trains, a situation only changed by the adding of a further island platform in the 1880s.

Several early companies built their station offices in classical style. One such was the Preston & Wyre. Its Lytham station is depicted, small but dignified with its high ceilings and pillared frontage. It formed the terminus of the branch from Kirkham from 16 February 1846 until the line was extended to Blackpool from 1 July 1874, and subsequently served as Lytham's goods station until its complete closure on 1 April 1963. The photograph was taken in April 1964.

Manchester Central was, in George Dow's words, 'all roof', and it lacked a building of suitable proportions to form a facade. This was not the original intention, for there was a scheme to build a CLC hotel embodying station buildings. In the event, the Midland built its own hotel beyond the station approaches and Central has continued to make do with the 'temporary' timber offices. Its closure is now imminent, but there are plans to preserve the roof for other purposes.

Overall roofs occur in many varieties of scale, design and materials. At Lytham (above) the modest train shed of the original station was supported by semi-circular timber arches. The Furness Railway was also fond of overall roofs. By far the most elaborate was at Barrow Central, completed in 1882 and destroyed during the air-raids of 1941. The south end (below) was photographed about 1910, with 4—4—0 33 of 1896 standing on the down line.

Like Manchester Victoria, Manchester London Road, or Piccadilly as it is now known, has undergone successive rebuildings and renamings. The overall roofs, however, have remained virtually unchanged since their completion in the rebuilding of 1881. In June 1951 ex-LMS Compound 41159 and ex-LNER C13 4—4—2 tank 67417 are standing in the former LNWR side of the station. On the far right are the former GCR platforms, separated by railings from the rest of the station and lettered rather than numbered.

By 1966 there have been many changes. The platforms have been completely relocated to give twelve terminal faces rather than ten. Electrification (at 1,500V DC on the GC side and 25,000V AC on the LNWR side) has revolutionised traction. The roof spans remain, but cleaning and redecoration has given them a new and fitting lightness.

From the middle of the nineteenth century, railway companies began to adopt standard designs for their buildings, for both economic and administrative reasons. Those of the Midland's Settle & Carlisle line are a classic instance, for though details and even materials may vary, almost every station has an assembly of buildings similar in both scale and design. At Ribblehead (left) there was a full range of buildings despite the isolated location. Until 1956, the booking hall was used for a monthly Sunday service, conducted by the Vicar of Ingleton. The mast beyond the building carries anemometer and wind vane, for the station, 1,025 ft high, has been a meteorological reporting point since 1938. The anemometer recorded a wind gust of 92 mph in November 1961, a reminder of the bleak nature of so much of the Settle & Carlisle route.

Many CLC stations also had a close family likeness. The basic H plan of the main building was similar to the Midland, but the stationmaster's house was included at one end of an asymmetric structure. Patterned brick and elaborately carved barge boards added to the cottage atmosphere. In November 1967, Type 2 diesel D 5277 passes the closed station at Baguley (below) on the Stockport-Altrincham line, with a train of limestone for ICI at Northwich. The large bay window of the station house, and the barge boards of the signal box are particularly striking.

Huyton station, about 1860, on the Liverpool & Manchester line, with a passenger train pulled by an Allan 'Crewe'-type 2—4—0. The short platforms and track almost buried in ballast were typical of the period. Most traces of this scene were obliterated when the line was quadrupled in 1871, and the right-hand buildings replaced by standard LNWR structures.

In contrast, the scene at Ormskirk, on the LYR Liverpool-Preston line is still largely unchanged since this photograph was taken at the turn of the century, with an Aspinall 4—4—0 entering on a Liverpool-bound train. Electrification (completed in 1913), a new footbridge (1966), a new awning on the down platform and upper quadrant signals mark the only changes of consequence apart from the length of ladies' skirts!

Pre-grouping signals still remain in some number, their variety a reminder of the complex antecedents of much of the railway network. At Denton Junction, on the Stockport-Stalybridge line, a Stalybridge-Stockport train passes a fine ex-LNWR specimen, its arms controlling, from left to right, the lines to Droylsden, Guide Bridge and Stalybridge respectively (opposite top).

Midland influence in the Peak is evident in both signal box and signals at Chinley East Junction. On a wintry January Sunday in 1966, the 9.30 am Liverpool Lime Street to Sheffield Midland train heads on to the Hope Valley line. Both box and signals have since been demolished, for the curve to the left is now closed (opposite bottom).

The iron horse begat iron in profusion, for iron was the prime material of the railway age. Cast-iron furnishings remain as a monument to Victorian solidity. On the CLC are these examples, a water column at Heaton Mersey shed (above) and a hydrant at Manchester Central (left). As usual, ownership is indelibly marked!

Creatures of the railway. The mythical Liver bird (top left) graces one of the piers of the bridge at Runcorn. At Brock, on the main line north of Preston, a badger decorates an overbridge (centre left). Rather better known, the lion at Glossop (below) cost the Duke of Norfolk £37 10s to crown the entrance to his station. The pigeons (top right) are an equally characteristic, and highly active, part of the Manchester Central scene.

Remaining links with the Lancashire & Yorkshire are found on the gatepost of Liverpool Exchange (left) and in the splendid departure indicator at Manchester Victoria (right). Company worthies perpetuated on company property were also an LYR characteristic. John Pearson (below left), portrayed at Liverpool Exchange, was chairman of the company as well as Mayor of Liverpool and High Sheriff of Lancashire. William Stuart (below right), who graces a bridge over Great Howard Street in Liverpool, was the company's deputy chairman 1849-59.

RAILWAY TOWNS

The railway was a tremendous stimulus to urban growth. In John Ruskin's vivid words, 'all vitality is concentrated through those throbbing arteries into the central cities; the country is passed over like a green sea by narrow bridges, and we are thrown back in continually closer crowds on the city gates.' But the railway was not only the arteries of an urban revolution, it directly fostered the creation of new types of town and the North West is particularly rich in examples of them; competing railway ports round Morecambe Bay, resorts dependent on railway links for their establishment and survival, railway workshops and the towns and suburbs which housed their labour.

The Furness Railway turned Barrow from a hamlet with a few farms and a population of less than 100 into a seething steel town of 60,000 in less than forty years. From the railway-developed port, with 700 acres of water and quay space, steamer services were established to the Isle of Man, Belfast and Fleetwood in partnership with the Midland until that company decided to build its own port at Heysham. Regular services ceased on the outbreak of war in 1914, but excursion boats continued until 1936. The photograph taken about 1930 shows the railway yards alongside Buccleuch Dock. Furness and LMS 0—6—0 tanks are shunting, while Isle of Man Steam Packet Company vessels are laid up alongside the quay. Beyond is a crane of Vickers' shipyard.

Sir Peter Hesketh-Fleetwood's plans for his new town at Fleetwood (page 24) included its development as a port, a development greatly stimulated by railway access and ownership, with steamer services to Glasgow (until 1848), Barrow, Ireland and the Isle of Man. The Isle of Man Steam Packet Company's vessels were the last passenger ships to sail from the port, being withdrawn in 1961. In 1964 (left) the cranes beyond the signals are demolishing the former passenger quay in the mouth of the Wyre. Fleetwood station itself was closed from 18 April 1966, services subsequently terminating at Wyre Dock.

The Lancashire & Yorkshire developed and owned the enclosed Wyre Dock from 1880 and the Fish Dock of 1908. Some general cargo is handled, but since 1897 Fleetwood has become primarily a fishing port, the largest on the west coast and the third largest in England and Wales. In 1933, deep sea trawlers unload at the covered market of the Fish Dock (left foreground) and lie at the coaling berths (right). Wyre Dock station is on the top left, and across Wyre Dock itself at the top right is the Lancashire & Yorkshire grain elevator, completed in 1882 with a capacity of 28,600 tons.

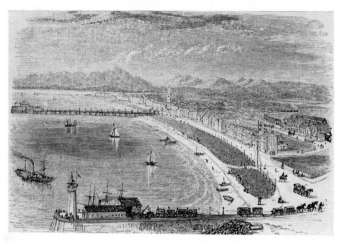

The Midland's bid for Irish Sea traffic centred on the Morecambe area. The 'little' North Western's line reached Poulton (as Morecambe was then known) on 12 June 1848, and by 1852 steamers were operating from the new pier. F. S. Williams' engraving (left), published in 1876, shows the rather inadequate stone jetty, with wagons being shunted by horse. The Town station of 1851 is on the right. Morecambe already shows substantial development as a resort with the inevitable iron pier and boarding houses lining the promenade.

In the 1890s, the Midland decided to create a new port at Heysham, three miles south of Morecambe. Initial plans were more ambitious than eventual reality. The quay in the foreground (below), photographed in the early 1930s, was to have formed a central pier, the land on the right being excavated for further docks, but even without this, the port had 3,000 ft of quay space when it opened in 1904. Unlike Barrow and Fleetwood, Heysham remains an important terminal for Irish traffic.

With the opening of Heysham, Morecambe became almost exclusively a resort. The former quay (left) now encloses the open-air swimming pool. The railway's importance to the resort was signified by the opening of the Midland's Promenade station on 24 March 1907 right on the sea front; the site of the former station was just in front of the overbridge. The LNWR's Euston Road station, to the left of the same bridge, was opened in 1886, but the Midland's influence remained dominant, not least in Morecambe's close association with visitors from Bradford and Leeds.

Blackpool is the archetype of the urban seaside resort, its development intimately linked with the railway's ability to carry large numbers swiftly and cheaply, not least from the industrial centres of east and south Lancashire. Its two terminals had more than three and a half miles of platform length: their capacity is symbolised by this view of Talbot Road station about 1896, its platforms filled with return Bass excursion trains for Burton-on-Trent. The rolling stock is Midland, but the locomotives LYR 4—4—0s of both large and small-wheeled varieties. The train on the extreme right is the Bass directors' special for St Pancras, and includes two Midland Pullmans in its formation.

In their heyday, railway workshops were a major source of employment. Horwich was a small cotton town of less than 4,000 people until the transfer of the LYR locomotive works from Miles Platting in 1887. By 1891, the total population of Horwich had risen to 12,850 and in 1894 the railway works employed over 3,000. In 1896, a line of Aspinall 2—4—2 tank engines near completion in the East Bay of the erecting shops (above).

The Manchester suburb of Gorton was formerly the location of two important locomotive works, Beyer Peacock's Gorton Foundry (1855-1966), and the Gorton Works of the Manchester, Sheffield & Lincolnshire, opened for repairs in 1848 and completing its first locomotive in March 1858. In 1963, four Class 9F 2—10—0s were among the last batch of engines to be overhauled in Gorton Works before its complete closure (below).

FREIGHT IN THE NORTH WEST

The North West generates a wide variety of freight traffic. Imported raw materials for its traditional industries move through Merseyside's docks. Coal, limestone and in earlier days iron ore are extracted from beneath its soil. Newer chemical and petrochemical industries provide bulk loads for contemporary block trains. In this section are a few glimpses of the area's characteristic freight.

An older order is symbolised at New Hey by the warehouse built by the Lancashire & Yorkshire for the storage of imported raw cotton. Now, with the cotton industry drastically contracted and much of its remaining traffic carried by road, the warehouse stands empty and devoid of tracks.

The former Great Central route from Manchester to Sheffield has long carried a heavy westbound movement of coal from the abundant pits of South Yorkshire to industrial Lancashire. In the early days of grouping, an ex-GC 2—8—0 (above) plods up towards Woodhead with an eastbound train of coal empties, the majority of them private-owner wagons.

Movement of coal over this route was eased by electrification in 1954, but long-term prospects must be viewed against the contraction of the coal industry and the transfer of energy in differing forms. In 1967, EM1 electric locomotive 26047 **Diomedes** descends from Woodhead with a westbound coal haul (below): behind is a pylon of the 275kV power line from the generating station at Thorpe Marsh (Doncaster) to Stalybridge, also carrying coal-derived energy. In the background of both photographs are Manchester's reservoirs in the Longdendale valley.

Little iron ore is now mined in the North West, but substantial quantities of imported ore are handled at the ports. One major flow is from the Bidston ore dock at Birkenhead to the John Summers steelworks at Hawarden Bridge, where blast furnaces were installed in 1953. Special wagons, each carrying sixty-five tons of ore, were built for the traffic. A Class 9F 2—10—0 enters the reception sidings at Hawarden Bridge with a load of ore (above); the steelworks itself lies beyond.

Coal production has declined drastically in South Lancashire. Agecroft is one of the few remaining collieries: diesel shunter D3588 is shunting in the colliery sidings (below). Much of the colliery's production of coal is fed direct to the adjacent power station.

Limestone is quarried at many locations along the Pennines, but the biggest concentration of such quarries clusters in the Peak District. At Tunstead, ICI quarries provide raw material for its chemical works at Northwich. A Class 4F 0—6—0 banks a train of loaded hoppers out of the ICI sidings into the short Great Rocks tunnel on the main Derby-Manchester line. The coal space in the tender is fitted with covers for protection from snow when the engine is engaged on snow plough duties. The line from the plant in the quarry itself passes through a deep cutting, having left the main line at Great Rocks Junction beyond the tunnel.

Modern freights in traditional settings. Class 9F 2—10—0 92094 winds a block train of oil empties from Yorkshire to Stanlow refinery past the mills of Dukinfield on the LNWR Stalybridge-Stockport line in September 1967.

Class 5 45135 drifts south past Grayrigg at the beginning of the descent to Oxenholme with a Larbert-Northwich ICI soda ash block train. On the right, sister engine 44778 on banking duties waits to drop down to Oxenholme after assisting a north-bound freight.

INDEPENDENTS

Until grouping merged its identity with the LMS, the Garstang & Knott End Railway provided railway service in the northern Fylde. Its first section was opened on 14 December 1870, though a chronic shortage of funds enabled it to give only a sporadic service in its early years. The second engine used on the line, **Union**, a Manning-Wardle 0—4—0 saddle tank of 1868 vintage, poses about 1875 at Garstang Town with one of the four original coaches (top). John Noble, the company's secretary and manager is on the end platform of the coach. The driver is James Stirzaker.

Blackpool (centre) was purchased from Manning-Wardle in 1909; its 2—6—0 wheel arrangement was unique for a standard-gauge tank engine in England. The carriages, with a transatlantic flavour, replaced the six-wheeled stock when the line finally reached Knott End in 1908.

Freight traffic survived as far as Pilling until 31 July 1963. On 13 August 1959, Class 5 45070 brings the daily freight, colloquially dubbed the 'Pilling Pig', into Garstang Town (bottom).

The Ravenglass & Eskdale Railway was built to tap the iron ore at the head of Eskdale, being opened for traffic on 24 May 1875. Narrow gauge was adopted to keep construction costs to a minimum. In 3 ft-gauge days, one of the line's two Manning-Wardle 0—6—0 tanks **Devon** waits with a passenger train at the former upper terminus at Boot about 1905 (top).

In its original form, the line expired in 1912, but from 1915 was revived after conversion to the 'miniature' 15 in gauge. On 4 August 1924, 4—4—2 **Sans Pareil** and 4—6—2 **Sir Aubrey Brocklebank** receive attention at the old station at Ravenglass after bringing in a double-headed train (centre).

The railway is now operated with the help of a Preservation Society, and its charm is captured in this scene (bottom). **River Irt**, unique for a tender engine in its 0—8—2 wheel arrangement, is leaving Dalegarth.

Liverpool's fourth main-line terminal, Riverside, was built for boat trains by the Mersey Docks & Harbour Board on the dock estate adjacent to the Princes Landing Stage; it was opened on 12 June 1895, when Liverpool was at the height of its status as a major passenger port for transatlantic traffic in particular. This view recalls a unique royal occasion in May 1951 when Queen Elizabeth travelled from London on a visit to Northern Ireland and Princess Margaret arrived in another train to join her. At the head of the two special trains are (left) 'Royal Scot' 46168 **The Girl Guide** and (right) Class 5 44911.

Both Manchester and Liverpool docks have extensive rail systems possessing a considerable stud of locomotives. Both are now completely dieselised, but at Manchester MSC 32, a Hudswell Clarke 0—6—0T built in 1903, shunts a train of cargo for Montreal alongside SS **Manchester Mariner** not long before its withdrawal from service on 6 July 1966. One of the last three steam locomotives, it had worked for some 300,000 hours covering about one million miles.

At Liverpool, MD & HB 39, a Hudswell Clarke 0 6—0 diesel built in 1963, runs on to the bridge at the entrance to Princes Dock. This route is used by boat trains from Riverside station, which lies beyond the shed on the right. The railway style signal controls traffic into the dock. Princes Dock is used for Irish traffic, the Dublin service from the left-hand quay and the Belfast service from the right. Beyond the dock is the Liver Building, completed in 1910, and one of the distinctive group of Liverpool's Pier Head buildings.

Many industrial concerns in the North West have extensive private railway systems. The scale of National Coal Board interests is suggested by this view of the interior of the workshops at Walkden, photographed in 1967. In the foreground are **Witch** and **Stanley**, two WD-pattern 0—6—0 saddle tanks, and immediately beyond, minus its saddle, another similar Hunslet engine. The last two are both fitted with Giesl ejectors for improving steaming. The third in the line on the left is another 0—6—0 tank, Robert Stephenson & Hawthorn 7739.

RAILWAY CONTRACTION

The contemporary railway is undergoing by far the greatest upheaval since its creation. Its near monopoly of inland transport has been completely broken and often painful readjustment is needed to fit it for a changing role. The contraction of services and of routes has been considerable, 'eliminating' in the words of the 1963 Beeching Report '. . . those services which, by their very nature, railways are ill-suited to provide.' Such changes have been far too extensive to illustrate in detail, but this section gives a few glimpses of the type of change which has taken place, change which will be ample grist for the future historian's mill.

'Last trains' have become almost a ritual, with packed coaches, engines garlanded with wreaths and a cacophony of detonators. Local services, both rural and urban, have been singularly vulnerable to road competition. Even before the sweeping Beeching proposals, closures were extensive: between 1950 and 1962 British Railways closed 4,236 route miles to passenger traffic. Some lines, however, go out with a whimper rather than a bang. On 1 November 1964, a night of thick fog, Class 4MT 4—6—0 75057 waits with only her crew for company at the head of the last train from Manchester Central to the former GCR terminus at Wigan Central, symbolising in more ways than one the end of an era.

After closure, the derelict line becomes an eyesore, of some interest to the industrial archaeologist, but of little value to local inhabitants. Not untypical is this September 1967 view from the remains of the signal box at Park Bridge, on the former Oldham, Ashton-under-Lyne & Guide Bridge Joint Railway, a scene of desolation and decay since final closure in February 1964.

Nature, however, given time has a softening hand. In sylvan surroundings are the remains of the bridge over the River Esk which carried a branch of the Ravenglass & Eskdale Railway from a point between Beckfoot and Boot to tap the iron ore deposits of the Ghyll Foss Drift. The branch was abandoned in 1877 with the failure of the Whitehaven Mining Company.

In other instances, the railway remains but its services are curtailed. On the line between Blackburn and Hellifield (see page 40), local passenger services were withdrawn from 10 September 1962, but the route remains an important link for through traffic between the Settle & Carlisle line and South Lancashire. Type 4 diesel D 1854 here heads the Sunday 10.30 am Glasgow to Birmingham train through the former Chatburn station on 6 August 1967, a regular Sunday diversion from the West Coast main line during engineering operations.

A particular source of traffic may save a railway from total abandonment Most of the former North Eastern Railway lines over Stainmore to Kirkby Stephen, Penrith and Tebay have been completely dismantled, but the section from Appleby to Merrygill remains to serve the latter's stone quarries. On 12 August 1966, Class 4MT 43040 passes the abandoned passenger station at Kirkby Stephen with the thrice weekly working to Merrygill. The vans in front of the tender are for Warcop Camp traffic.

Lavish facilities provided in the high noon of railway development may no longer be required for reduced or more efficiently operated traffic. The LNWR route from Stalybridge to Huddersfield over Standedge ultimately provided four tracks all the way, but this is no longer necessary. On 25 February 1966 English Electric Type 4 diesel D256 leaves the double track tunnel at Standedge with the 8.42 am Newcastle-Liverpool train. The two earlier single track bores on the right were closed to traffic on 30 October 1966; the left hand of the two was the original tunnel of 1849 (see page 32).

Local freight services have also been curtailed and many small goods yards closed in favour of more centralised handling. At Shaw and Crompton, the now-demolished LYR warehouse still remained on 8 September 1967, the mill beyond a reminder of its former role, but the tracks which served it and the extensive goods yard in the foreground have all been lifted.

Some railway formations and railway structures now serve an entirely different purpose from that for which they were designed. All services were withdrawn at Skelmersdale, on the former LYR Rainford-Ormskirk line, from 4 November 1963 shortly after the photograph was taken (top). The formation has now been converted into a road serving the new town; in July 1967 construction was under way, but the crossing gates and goods shed still survived (centre).

At Southport, the former CLC line was an early candidate for closure, services being withdrawn from 7 July 1952. Part of the formation at Ainsdale has also been used for a road: the terminus at Lord Street now serves as a bus station, 'platform' being given a totally new connotation (bottom).

RAILWAY ADVANCE

Somewhat undeservedly, railway contraction tends to hit the headlines rather than railway advance. But route rationalisation, the renovation and replacement of structures, new methods of freight handling and new traffic flows, electrification and resignalling also create startling changes in the railway landscape. Changes of this kind are found throughout the North West, though the most far-reaching are concentrated on the conurbations to the south and their links with the Midlands and London.

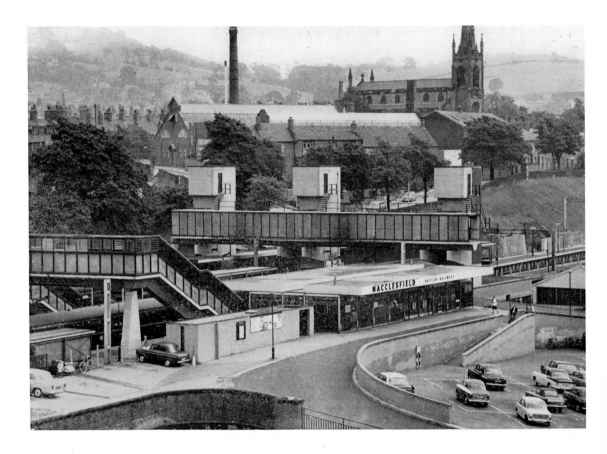

Many towns contain two or more stations, the legacy of earlier competition and duplication. Rationalisation is not always straightforward, but several such opportunities have been grasped. At Macclesfield, two stations existed, the ex-LNWR Hibel Road, and the ex-North Staffordshire Central. Traffic could conveniently be concentrated on the site of Central, and the completely rebuilt premises were opened on 7 November 1960 as Macclesfield's sole station.

The emergence of Manchester Piccadilly has already been described (page 75). The latest development has involved the complete replacement of the former terminal buildings. Even though re-signed in early British Railways style, in June 1951 (above) the booking office windows were still Victorian in aspect, the booking clerks almost hidden beyond the cave-like windows. Above, the carved crest of the original Manchester & Birmingham Railway is a tangible reminder of the line's origins. The completeness of change is evident below, with glass replacing panelled wood and multiprinter machines the serried ranks of printed tickets. At long last too, logic has overtaken the accidents of history, and second class replaces third.

Freightliners have brought the containerisation of trunk merchandise hauls. Brush Type 4 diesel D1840 drops down from Grayrigg, just past Lambrigg, with an up Freightliner in July 1967. In the background, the fells on the eastern edge of the Lake District point to the difficulties of the climb over Shap beyond.

At Liverpool, the Freightliner depot has been built on the former LNWR dock estate at Garston. The cranes of the docks themselves can be seen beyond the houses, while in the background is the estuary of the Mersey and industrial Bromborough. Freightliner flats stand on both roads and on the left is the crane for transferring containers to road vehicles.

The Ford Motor Company, unable to expand on their existing site at Dagenham, have built a vast new assembly plant at Halewood, on the outskirts of Liverpool adjacent to the main London railway. Three trains, each with twenty-six specially designed vans, run a daily shuttle service between Halewood and Dagenham, forming virtually an extension of the company's assembly lines. Here V4 engines from Dagenham are being unloaded at Halewood. Block loads of this character are particularly suitable for rail haulage.

The most startling changes have come with the electrification at 25kV AC of the main lines to the south from Manchester and Liverpool. Electrification necessarily brought substantial reconstruction, and often radically altered former landmarks. The railway bridge over Hyde Road on the route out of Manchester London Road was the scene of the rescue on 18 September 1867 of two Fenian leaders from the police van in which they were travelling (above). In the ensuing scuffle, one of the police escort was fatally wounded, a crime for which the three 'Manchester Martyrs', Allen, Larkin and O'Brien, were subsequently hanged. During reconstruction (below) all traces of the original 'Fenian Arches' were removed, with pre-stressed concrete girders now spanning the whole roadway.

Electrification involved far more than the installation of overhead power supplies and track relaying. The opportunity was also taken for complete resignalling. Control of the whole line between Manchester and Crewe, for example, was concentrated in three signal boxes only, at Piccadilly, Wilmslow and Sandbach. At Wilmslow, the small ex-LNWR structure (above) was replaced by a large new box (right) whose control panel (below) covers fourteen miles of route and thirty-one miles of track, from Chelford to Cheadle Hulme, and to Gatley on the Styal line.

The scale of change in the railway scene is symbolised by this view of a Liverpool-Euston express on the approaches to Runcorn viaduct in June 1967. Five miles to the north, at Rainhill, Stephenson's **Rocket** startled contemporaries on 8 October 1829 by averaging about sixteen mph and momentarily reaching twenty-nine. Traffic over the Liverpool & Manchester grew to such an extent that the Runcorn line itself was opened to ease congestion and speed London traffic in 1869; its serried arches and lattice girder spans reveal a confident engineering mastery. Now with electrification, expresses such as this bring London within 2 h 32 m of Liverpool, travelling at sustained speeds of one hundred mph with start to stop averages in excess of eighty.

SOURCES OF ILLUSTRATIONS AND ACKNOWLEDGMENTS

Liverpool Record Office collection, 8, 18, 19 (top, bottom), 20, 21 (top, bottom), 22 (middle, bottom), 23 (top, bottom), 49 (top, bottom)

Manchester Central Library collection, 9, 37 (top), 51 (top), 106 (bottom)

Aerofilms Ltd, 11, 51 (bottom), 54, 68, 70, 84 (bottom)

Preston Scientific Society, Record and Survey Committee collection, 12 (bottom)

E. R. Morten and Brian Lamb collections, 13 (top)

E. R. Morten, 16 (top), 57, 59 (middle), 90

BR London Midland Region, 16 (bottom), 27 (middle, bottom), 45 (middle, bottom), 46 (top), 48 (bottom), 50 (middle, bottom), 62, 74 (bottom), 75 (top, bottom), 82, 83 (bottom), 84 (bottom), 85 (bottom), 86 (top), 89 (top), 103 (top), 105 (top), 107 (top left, bottom)

T. J. Edgington, 17 (top, middle)

John Marshall, 23 (middle), 37 (bottom), 43 (bottom), 73 (top), 74 (top)), 81 (top left, bottom left, bottom right), 83 (top), 101 (top)

Frank Walmsley collection, 27 (top), 92 (top)

Frank Walmsley, 92 (bottom)

L. J. Thompson, 29 (middle)

R. L. Sewell, 29 (bottom), 44 (top)

R. E. Toop, 42, 44 (bottom), 45 (top)

W. Hardin Osborne, 43 (top)

Liverpool Museums collection, by permission of the Liverpool Libraries, Museums and Arts Committee, 48 (top), 77 (top)

Real Photographs Co Ltd, 48 (middle), 60 (bottom)

Douglas Doherty, 52 (bottom)

W. Oliver, 53 (top)

Phil Murray, 59 (bottom)

Brian Lister, 63 (top, bottom), 64

Isaac Hailwood, 65 (bottom)

D. A. Halsall collection, 77 (bottom)

Airviews (Manchester) Ltd, 85 (top)

K. Hoole collection, 88 (top)

Locomotive Publishing Co Ltd, 92 (middle)

Mary C. Fair and Ravenglass & Eskdale Railway, 93 (top, middle)

Mersey Docks and Harbour Board, 94, 95 (bottom)

Port of Manchester, 95 (top)

Ford Motor Company Ltd, 105 (bottom)

Liverpool University Library collection, 106 (top)

All other illustrations are from the authors' collections or photographs taken by the authors

All maps were drawn by Mr A. G. Hodgkiss of the Department of Geography, University of Liverpool

The authors are most grateful for all the help and ready co-operation they have received from the photographers and others listed above. They would also like to thank the following for their interest and assistance:

Mr P. D. Pocklington, Chester Public Library
Mr N. Carrick, Liverpool Record Office
Mr E. W. Paget-Tomlinson, Keeper of Shipping, City of Liverpool Museums
The staff of Manchester Central Library
Miss Hilda Lofthouse, Chetham's Library, Manchester
Miss Jane A. Downton, The Harris Public Library, Preston
The Divisional Public Relations and Publicity Officers, British Rail, Liverpool and Manchester
The District Engineer's office, British Rail, Manchester
Messrs G. Collins, W. J. K. Davies, J. P. Feather, D. Ferreira, G. F. Flower, G. Hall, G. O. Holt, D. Joy, R. S. Patterson, C. H. Shepherd, and R. J. Smirk

INDEX